Essential Question
How can we understand nature?

WHY TURTLES LIVE IN WATER

by Deborah November
illustrated by Linda Bittner

CAST OF CHARACTERS

Little Turtle

Turtle Friend I

Turtle Friend 2

Hunter I

Hunter 2

Chief

SCENE 1

LIFE OF THE TURTLE

Setting: A long time ago in faraway Africa

Little Turtle: What a lovely day!

Turtle Friend I: Yes, life is good.

Turtle Friend 2: We live a happy life playing in the tall grass.

Little Turtle: And we always have plenty to eat.

3

Turtle Friend 1: Some hunters are coming! Hurry and hide!

Turtle Friend 2: Little Turtle, run as fast as you can!

STOP AND CHECK

Where do the turtles like to play?

4

CAPTURE!

Setting: A path in the jungle

Hunter I: We have you, Little Turtle!

Hunter 2: Don't try to dash away. It is too late.

Little Turtle: Oh my goodness! The hunters were so fast I did not even have a chance to holler! I am filled with fear.

Little Turtle: I am ashamed that the hunters caught me.

Hunter I: No talking, Little Turtle!

STOP AND CHECK

Who caught Little Turtle?

7

THE VILLAGE

Setting: The hunters' village

Hunter 2: Here we are in our village.

Little Turtle: I don't want to look!

8

Chief: I am the chief of this village. Welcome, Little Turtle!

Little Turtle:
Thank you, sir!

Chief: How shall we cook him?

Little Turtle: You will have to take me out of this shell.

Chief: We'll break your shell with sticks.

Little Turtle: You have great wisdom, Chief, but that won't work. Why don't you throw me in the river and drown me?

Chief: Good idea, Little Turtle. Soon we will celebrate our victory. We will drown the turtle!

STOP AND CHECK

What did the animals of the village want to do to the turtle?

SCENE 4

ESCAPE!

Setting: The hunters' village

Little Turtle: I don't want to boast, but I would not get those cooking pots out too fast!

Hunter I: He tricked us!

Chief: The turtle is getting away!

Little Turtle: I think I'll spend most of my time safely in the water from now on.

Turtle Friend I: Little Turtle is home and safe!

Turtle Friend 2: Let's have a party!

Turtle Friend I: And that is why turtles live in water.

STOP AND CHECK

What did Little Turtle say after he landed in the river?

Respond to Reading

Summarize

Use details to summarize *Why Turtles Live in Water.*

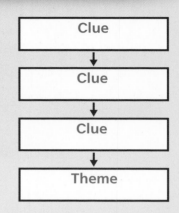

Text Evidence

1. How do you know *Why Turtles Live in Water* is a folktale? Genre

2. How does Little Turtle get away from the hunters? Theme

3. What is the root word of *getting* on page 14? Root Words

4. Write how this folktale explains nature. Write About Reading

Compare Texts
Read to find out why corn has silk.

Why Corn Has Silk

Long ago, a man lived alone. He grew food to eat. The man was worried. He did not know if he had enough food for the winter. Then he saw a woman coming.

The woman wanted to help him. She told him to rub sticks together. He could make fire that way. She said that seeds grow better in ground that is burned. Then she said to carry her across the field.

He carried the woman. Her long yellow hair hit the ground. When the corn was ready, the woman's yellow hair was the silk in the corn. The man saw the similarities. That is why corn has silk.

Make Connections

What explains why corn has silk?
Essential Question

How do these two folktales explain nature? Text to Text

Focus on
Literary Elements

Theme The theme is the lesson or message in a story or play.

What to Look for In the play, the author tells you why turtles live in water. Look for what Little Turtle did. How did he end up in the water? What is the lesson?

Your Turn

Plan a play about an animal. Make a list of details to include in your play. Include where the animal lives. Include how it got its home.